Birds of the Midwest

Stan Tekiela

Adventure Quick Guides

YOUR WAY TO EASILY IDENTIFY BACKYARD BIRDS

Adventure Quick Guides

Organized by color for quick and easy identification, this guide covers 113 species of the most common birds found in the Midwest. *Water Birds of the Midwest* and *Birds of Prey of the Midwest* together include an additional 133 species for a total of 246 species represented in these three Midwest Quick Guides.

KEY

- If the male and female of a species look the same or nearly the same, only one bird is shown.

- When the male and female are different colors, they are shown in their respective color sections with "male" or "female" labels.

- The smaller type indicates the color section in which the male/female counterpart is found.

- A feeder icon ♜ indicates the bird visits backyard feeders.

Northern Cardinal
black mask, red bill

male red
female

MIDWEST BIRD FIELD GUIDES

For more information about nesting, young, migration and interesting gee-whiz facts, use Stan's field guides for these Midwest states: the Dakotas, Illinois, Indiana, Iowa, Kansas, Kentucky, Michigan, Minnesota, Missouri, Nebraska, Ohio and Wisconsin.

MIDWEST PLAYING CARDS

STAN TEKIELA

Stan Tekiela is an award-winning photographer, naturalist and author of over 190 field guides, nature books, children's books and more about birds, mammals, reptiles, amphibians, trees and wildflowers.

15 14 13 12 11

Birds of the Midwest
Copyright © 2013 by Stan Tekiela
Published by Adventure Publications
An imprint of AdventureKEEN
All rights reserved
Printed in China
ISBN 978-1-59193-406-6

Cover and book design by Lora Westberg
Edited by Sandy Livoti
Cover image by Stan Tekiela:
    Eastern Bluebird

All images copyrighted. Images by Stan Tekiela and contributing photographers: Kevin T. Karlson, Maslowski Wildlife Productions and Brian E. Small.

Blue-gray Gnatcatcher

blue gray with dark forehead

Indigo Bunting

blue with dark wings

female brown

male

Lazuli Bunting

turquoise head, rusty chest

female brown

male

Tree Swallow

white chin and chest

Eastern Bluebird

sky blue with rusty chest, female duller

Mountain Bluebird

deep blue, female paler

Blue Grosbeak

rusty wing bars

female brown

male

Barn Swallow

orange forehead, forked tail, female duller

4"   5 1/2"   5 1/2"   5 1/2"   7"   7"   7"   7"

Mostly blue

Purple Martin

female

Purple Martin
nearly black,
notched tail,
female gray belly

male

Blue Jay
blue crest,
black necklace

Belted Kingfisher
shaggy crest,
female has
two bands
on chest

Mostly yellow

female

American Goldfinch
male
black forehead,
female lacks
black forehead

American Redstart
yellow
patches,
white belly
female
male orange

Kentucky Warbler
black
cap, yellow
around eye

Magnolia Warbler
black necklace,
thick streaks
on chest, female
less black

8 1/2"   12"   13"   5"   5"   5"   5"

Mostly yellow

Prairie Warbler
chestnut streaks on back

Yellow Warbler
orange streaks on chest, female lacks streaks

Common Yellowthroat
black mask, female lacks mask

Palm Warbler
chestnut cap, yellow eyebrows

female

Dickcissel
black bib, female lacks bib

male

Red Crossbill
dull yellow, long crossed bill

female

male red

Bobolink
pale nape, dark forehead, thin eye line

male black

female

Scarlet Tanager
yellowish with dark wings

male red

female

5"   5"   5"   5 1/2"   6"   6 1/2"   7"   7"

Mostly yellow

female

Western Tanager

yellow with red head, black wings, female olive wings

male

Baltimore Oriole

pale yellow, white wing bars

female

male orange

Orchard Oriole

dull yellow, white wing bars

male orange

female

female

Evening Grosbeak

bright yellow eyebrows, large ivory bill, female duller

male

Summer Tanager

large bill

male red

female

Western Kingbird

yellow belly, dark tail

Eastern Meadowlark

black V on chest, white outer tail feathers as seen in flight

Western Meadowlark

black V on chest, white outer tail feathers as seen in flight

7 1/4"   7 1/2"   7 1/2"   8"   8"   9"   9"   9"

Ruby-crowned Kinglet

white
wing bars

Red-breasted Nuthatch

black eye line,
female
gray cap

Black-capped Chickadee

black cap,
white cheeks,
white wing edges

Carolina Chickadee

black cap, gray cheeks,
gray wing edges

Boreal Chickadee

brown cap

Dark-eyed Junco

white belly,
pink bill

male   female brown

White-breasted Nuthatch

black cap,
white cheeks,
female
duller cap

Yellow-rumped Warbler

white chin, bold
yellow
patches,
female duller

4"   4 1/2"   5"   5"   5 1/2"   5 1/2"   5 1/2"   5 1/2"

Yellow-throated Warbler

yellow chin, black face, female duller

Tufted Titmouse

large crest

Eastern Phoebe

pumps tail up and down while perched

Great Crested Flycatcher

yellow belly, long rusty tail

Eastern Kingbird

white-tipped tail

Gray Catbird

chestnut patch under tail

Pine Grosbeak

yellow-tinged head, white wing bars

male red

female

Loggerhead Shrike

black mask

5 1/2"   6"   7"   8"   8"   9"   9"   9"

Mostly gray

Northern Mockingbird
long tail, white wing bars

American Robin
black head, female gray head

Canada Jay
white forehead

Rock Pigeon
variety of colors

Mostly orange

American Redstart
orange patches

female yellow

male

Baltimore Oriole
male

black head, white wing bars

female yellow

Orchard Oriole
black head, rusty body

female yellow

male

10"   10"   11 1/2"   13"   5"   7 1/2"   7 1/2"

House Finch

brown cap

female brown

Purple Finch

red cap

female brown

male

male

Red Crossbill

long crossed bill

female yellow

Scarlet Tanager

black wings
and tail

female yellow

male

male

Summer Tanager

overall red

female yellow

Northern Cardinal

black mask,
red crest, red bill

female brown

male

male

Pine Grosbeak

two white wing bars

female gray

male

5"   6"   6 1/2"   7"   8"   8 1/2"   9"

Mostly brown

Brown Creeper
long curved bill

House Finch
brown cap, streaked flanks and belly

male red

female

Common Redpoll
red cap, red wash on chest, female lacks red wash

Pine Siskin
yellow streaks on wings, female less yellow

Chipping Sparrow
rusty cap, clear chest

Chimney Swift
pointed head and tail as seen in flight

Chestnut-sided Warbler
yellow cap, chestnut sides, female duller

House Wren
short curved bill

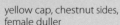

5"   5"   5"   5"   5"   5"   5"   5"

Mostly brown

Indigo Bunting
brown with lighter throat

male blue

female

Lazuli Bunting
two narrow wing bars

male blue

female

Dark-eyed Junco
brown with white belly

male gray

female

Song Sparrow
central dark spot on streaked chest

Cliff Swallow
tan-to-rust forehead and cheeks

Carolina Wren
white eyebrows, white markings on sides of neck

Purple Finch
white eye stripe

male red

female

Chestnut-collared Longspur
rusty nape, white and yellow throat, female duller

5 1/2"   5 1/2"   5 1/2"   5 1/2"   5 1/2"   5 1/2"   6"   6"

American Tree Sparrow

rusty cap, central dark spot on clear chest

House Sparrow

female

black throat, gray cap, female tan eyebrows

male

female

Lapland Longspur

black head, yellow bill, female lacks black head

male

Lark Bunting

heavily streaked with two bold stripes on throat

female

male black & white

Lark Sparrow

bold head pattern, central dark spot on white chest

White-throated Sparrow

white chin, bold eyebrows

Blue Grosbeak

brown with tan wing bars

male blue

female

Fox Sparrow

heavily streaked chest and belly

6"   6"   6 1/2"   6 1/2"   6 1/2"   6 1/2"   7"   7"

Mostly brown

White-crowned Sparrow

black and white head

Swainson's Thrush

brown spots on chin, chest and belly

Brown-headed Cowbird

whitish throat

male black

Rose-breasted Grosbeak

bold white eyebrows

female

male black & white

Horned Lark

white-to-yellow throat, black necklace, female duller

Harris's Sparrow

black and gray head

Eastern Towhee

rusty sides, red eyes

male black

female

Cedar Waxwing

black mask, red wing tips

7"   7"   7 1/2"   7 1/2"   7 1/2"   7 1/2"   7 1/2"   7 1/2"

Wood Thrush
rusty head, black spots on chest and belly

Bohemian Waxwing
black mask, white and red wing tips

Red-winged Blackbird
light eyebrows

male black

female

Northern Cardinal
black mask, red bill

male red

female

Spotted Towhee
female

brown head, red eyes

male black

Common Nighthawk
white chin, white band across wings as seen in flight, female tan chin

Yellow-headed Blackbird
dull yellow head and chest

male black

female

Northern Bobwhite
white eyebrows and chin, female tan eyebrows and chin

8"   8 1/4"   8 1/2"   8 1/2"   8 1/2"   9"   10"   10"

Mostly brown

Whip-poor-will

large dark eyes, gray on back

Killdeer

two black bands around neck

Brown Thrasher

long tail, long curved bill

Yellow-billed Cuckoo

white chin, dark bars on long tail

Mourning Dove

blue eye-ring, bobs head while walking

Northern Flicker

yellow wing linings, black mark on face, female lacks black mark

Greater Prairie-Chicken

yellow skin above eyes, short wide tail

Ruffed Grouse

dark ruffs

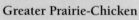

10"   11"   11"   12"   12"   12"   17"   17 1/2"

Mostly brown

Great-tailed Grackle
long tail, white eyes

female

male black

Ring-necked Pheasant
long tail, white ring around neck, female all brown

female

male

female

Wild Turkey
bare skin on head, black beard, female lacks beard

male

Mostly black & white

Black-and-white Warbler
black throat and cheeks, female lacks black patches

Downy Woodpecker
short bill, red spot, female lacks red spot

Lark Bunting
white wing bar

female brown

male

Snow Bunting
white with black and rusty highlights

18"   33"   42"   5"   6"   6 1/2"   7"

Rose-breasted Grosbeak

rose chest patch

female brown

male

Yellow-bellied Sapsucker

red cap and chin, female white chin and throat

Hairy Woodpecker

large bill, red spot, female lacks red spot

Red-headed Woodpecker

red head

Red-bellied Woodpecker

red cap and nape, female gray cap

Scissor-tailed Flycatcher

pink wing linings, long tail, female shorter tail

Pileated Woodpecker

red crest and mustache, female black forehead

Black-billed Magpie

black bill, long tail, female shorter tail

7 1/2"   8 1/2"   9"   9"   9 1/4"   10"   19"   20"

Mostly black

Bobolink

yellow nape, white shoulders and rump

female yellow

male

Brown-headed Cowbird

brown head, gray bill

male

female brown

European Starling

bill yellow in summer, gray in winter

Eastern Towhee

black head and chest, red eyes

female brown

male

Red-winged Blackbird

red and yellow shoulder patches

female brown

male

Spotted Towhee

white spots on back, red eyes

female brown

male

Yellow-headed Blackbird

yellow head, white wing patches

female brown

male

Common Grackle

blue head, long tail, female shorter tail

7"   7 1/2"   7 1/2"   7 1/2"   8 1/2"   8 1/2"   10"   12"

American Crow

black with familiar "caw" call

Great-tailed Grackle

purple head, long tail, yellow eyes

male

female brown

Common Raven

shaggy throat feathers

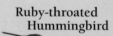

Mostly green

Ruby-throated Hummingbird

ruby throat, female lacks ruby throat

18"   18"   24 1/2"   3 1/4"

Bird Feeding Guide

Bluebirds

Favorite: mealworms
Also: dried fruit

Cardinals

Favorite: black oil sunflower seeds
Also: striped sunflower seeds, safflower, millet, cracked corn,
peanut butter

Chickadees, Nuthatches & Titmice

Favorite: black oil sunflower seeds
Also: striped sunflower seeds, safflower, millet, Nyjer thistle,
peanut butter, suet, shelled peanuts, nectar, cracked
corn, mealworms, fruit

Doves

Favorite: millet
Also: cracked corn, safflower, hulled sunflower seeds, milo

Finches (including Grosbeaks & Crossbills)

Favorite: Nyjer thistle
Also: millet, black oil sunflower seeds, striped sunflower seeds,
hulled sunflower seeds, cracked corn, safflower, orange
halves, grape jelly

Hummingbirds

Favorite: nectar

Jays & Crows

Favorite: grape jelly
Also: shelled peanuts, black oil sunflower seeds, peanut butter,
whole or cracked corn, bread crumbs, dried fruit, suet, milo

Orioles

Favorite: grape jelly
Also: orange halves, mealworms, nectar

Sparrows (including Juncos & Towhees)

Favorite: cracked corn
Also: millet, black oil sunflower seeds, striped sunflower
seeds, hulled sunflower seeds, safflower

Woodpeckers (including Flickers & Sapsuckers)

Favorite: suet
Also: shelled peanuts, nuts, acorns, peanut butter, black oil
sunflower seeds, mealworms, dried fruit, orange halves,
whole corn, grape jelly

Adventure Quick Guides

Only Midwest Birds
Organized by color
for quick and easy identification

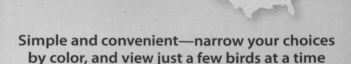

Simple and convenient—narrow your choices by color, and view just a few birds at a time

- Pocket-sized format—easier than laminated foldouts

- Professional photos showing key markings

- Bird feeder icon and feeding guide

- Silhouettes and sizes for quick comparison

- Based on Stan Tekiela's best-selling bird field guides

Get these great *Adventure Quick Guides* for the Midwest

ISBN 978-1-59193-406-6

$9.95

5 0 9 9 5

9 781591 934066

Adventure
PUBLICATIONS
an imprint of AdventureKEEN

NATURE/BIRDS/MIDWEST